The

Customer

Stream

The
Customer
Stream

15 Innovative and Unique Strategies Local Business Owners Can Use To Keep New Customers Flowing In The Door and Get Customers To Come Back and Spend More Money

Doug Anderson

Published by Doug Anderson, 26 E 2nd St, Litchfield, MN 55355 Phone 1-855-693-0699

Printed in the United States of America

ISBN-13: 978-1467918916
ISBN-10: 1467918911

This book is dedicated to all the small business owners who recognize that good marketing is the key to their success and are willing to take steps to implement it in their business.

About The Author

Doug Anderson has over 30 years sales, marketing and business experience.

He has been helping small businesses with the techniques laid out in this book since 2007.

As a customer service manager for a previous employer he helped the company grow from 1.2 million dollars in revenue to over 35 million when he left.

He and his wife Marjie just celebrated their 30th Anniversary in October 2011. Together they have 2 grown sons and one granddaughter. They reside in a small town just west of Minneapolis Minnesota.

Doug is the owner of New Customers Now! Minnesota, a Direct Marketing company. He is an expert at filling local businesses with new customers, getting them to return, and getting them to spend more money each visit.

To speak with Doug about your business, please call **1-855-693-0699** or visit **www.TheCustomerStream.com.**

FREE CONSULT!

To speak with Doug Anderson about filling your local business with new customers, getting them to come back, and getting them to spend more money each visit:

Please Call **1-855-693-0699** or Visit **www.TheCustomerStream.com**

Foreword

I'd like to congratulate you on obtaining Doug's book, *The Customer Stream.* I believe this is one of the most innovative books on filling a local business with customers that you will ever read.

There are many books on the market that teach you ways to market your local business, many of them re-treads of ideas you already know. There are books filled with bright, shiny tactics that promise to bring you rich rewards with little or no work. And seemingly, all you seem to read about is the Internet and Mobile Phones being the only way to fill your local business these days.

Me personally, I'm much less impressed by theory and "all things new". I'm enamored by results. That's why I'm so glad to have met Doug Anderson and am recommending that you read this book. Doug's ideas produce proven results. That's what we all want for our business – proven results.

I believe what you are about to learn is brilliant in its simplicity. The ideas which you will be presented are amongst the most creative strategies I've ever seen at filling a local business with paying customers that not only buy from you once, but will return again and again, spending more than ever before.

This book is not about being tricky or mastering persuasion. This book is about being original, creative, and entertaining. Doug will show you how he's achieved outstanding results for his clients and his own business using media which people have written off, forgotten about, or simply never considered.

In this book, Doug shows you campaigns that get more people to respond, more people to visit, more people to spend, more people to refer, and more people to become regular customers than anything you've seen before.

The creativity of these strategies will inspire you, and the results Doug shows you from actual campaigns should motivate you to try these strategies in your own business.

Whether you run a dry cleaning business, an accounting firm, a restaurant, a chiropractic office, a salon, an auto repair shop, a financial practice, a bar, or even a pet supply store, Doug's strategies will help you get the customer stream you've dreamed about.

I challenge you to carve out time to read this book and apply the strategies Doug reveals here. I'd also encourage you to take advantage of the resources that Doug makes available, including consulting time to pick his brain (because he's always thinking of new ideas). I'm astonished as an experienced marketer at the results Doug's strategies produce. I can't wait to hear more success stories from Doug.

I hope you enjoy this book as much as I did, and I wish you tremendous success in your business!

Bob Regnerus is the author of Big Ticket eCommerce and Co-Host of The Game Changers Radio Show on AM560-WIND in Chicago.

Table Of Contents

INTRODUCTION

There are only three ways to grow a business:

1. Bring in new customers

2. Get existing customers to come back more often

3. Get customers to spend more in each transaction

Customers are your life blood. You need people who are willing to spend their hard-earned money to use your products or services. Whatever you call them – customers, clients, consumers, or patients – without these folks you don't have a business. Generating a stream of customers for your business is a constant requirement.

Advertising usually is the prescribed solution. Sadly, much advertising is largely non-productive and wasteful. Most business owners have no idea how well (or how poorly) their marketing efforts are working to bring customers in the door because most owners have no system in place to track actual returns on their marketing strategies. Without knowing your numbers, you could be wasting hundreds and thousands of dollars each and every month.

In their attempt to create a customer stream, a common approach busy small business owners take is "I'll run an ad in the newspaper or radio and hope that will work" or "If I set up a website and get listed online, I can steer them in through that."

Let me ask you, do you know exactly how many customers came in from that last ad on the radio or in the newspaper? Do you know how many clients were generated by your online listing or website? Are you truly reaching the best demographic for your business? Just as important, do you have any means of getting those who come in once to come back again?

The truth is that old school marketing tactics -- Yellow Pages, radio, newspaper ads – are really scatter-shot and are not very cost-effective. The latest internet marketing fad, daily deal site, or coupon won't cure all your ills. If not managed appropriately, these strategies all tend to be just as untargeted and costly to you. No strategy is going to be useful to you if you can't assess what's working or not.

What this type of effort amounts to is marketing via hope, as in, "I hope this ad works." Aaargh! **Hope is not a marketing strategy.** Unfortunately it's what most business owners rely on. Is it any wonder that so many small businesses fail within the first five years?

Obviously, you have to advertise to acquire new customers. You have to bring in a steady stream of new customers, not only to grow the business, but to replace the customers that you lose. I like to say that every business, whether you admit it or not, is like a bucket full of holes. You are constantly losing customers like a leaky bucket even though many are lost through no fault of your own. Changes occur in your customers' lives. They move, give birth, retire, and, eventually, die. Sometimes customers are lost through some perceived neglect on your part, either because of inattention while they are customers, or simply not keeping in touch with them after the fact. If you don't remind customers that you exist, they forget about you.

One of the most overlooked assets in your business is your existing customers. They're far more valuable and less costly to you than a new customer. You should be investing in retaining your existing customers as much or even more than you do on getting new customers in the door. According to the Harvard Business Review, an increase in customer retention of 5% can yield an increase in profits by 25% to 85%!

If you can get a customer to come back and do business with you a second time, there's a good chance they will become a repeat customer again in the near future. There are many things you can do to encourage this, but don't be like a lot of business owners and believe people will automatically remember you and come back in. *It's not your customer's job to remember to do business with you; it's your job to remind them!* Don't fall for the delusion that because you provided a good experience they'll never forget you. People forget! They have a lot going on in their lives...and your competition is right around the corner, ready to give them more reasons to forget you.

Now, if the picture I've painted for you seems bleak, don't worry. It's not bad news for you, it's bad news for your competition. While they continue to use hope as their marketing strategy, you're going to be equipped with new ideas and strategies that work *in any economy*. I will show you a way of advertising that is predictable, accountable, and highly responsive. Simply put, **these strategies produce a customer stream and revenue** – exactly what you're looking for!

These marketing strategies are geared towards bringing in a steady stream of new customers, keeping in contact with those who have already done business with you, and getting customers to spend more money on each visit. These strategies are unique, fun, and memorable. These have been proven to work because these strategies all provide ways to directly track and measure the results in terms of customers, costs, and revenue.

I've personally worked through these strategies with clients just like you and helped them climb out of their rut. By using what I am going to reveal to you in this book, you can expect healthy returns on your investment. Some clients are achieving response rates of 20%, 30%, 40% to 50% and higher using the same strategies you'll read about!

As you read about these direct response marketing strategies, imagine how they can be implemented in your business. A strategy I reveal using a restaurant, for example, can be used in your business too, even if you don't own a restaurant. Think creatively. These strategies have worked with many small businesses – restaurants, dental offices, auto repair services, beauty shops, dry cleaners, and many more.

These marketing tactics and strategies have been so successful, they've been featured in two books: <u>Outrageous Advertising That's Outrageously Successful</u> by Bill Glazer and <u>No BS Marketing to the Affluent</u> by Dan Kennedy.

As those book titles might suggest, the strategies involve thinking outside of the box and finding fun (and unusual) approaches to marketing that get prospects interested and turn them into customers, clients and patients. These marketing methods are so fun and unique, they'll even get customers talking to their friends about your business.

So get out your highlighter, open up your notebook, and get away to a quiet place. I want you to absorb these ideas and use them in your business. No strategy can work if it remains an idea. You need to implement these strategies to make them work for you! And I want to hear about your success.

Before you read any further, I invite you to visit an important website. While I will describe all these strategies in detail for you in this book, to fully appreciate them you need to see them in full color. To do this, I've created a special website just for you.

Please visit **www.TheCustomerStream.com** and there you will be given exclusive access to full color examples, resources that accompany this book, and all my latest and greatest strategies which I am constantly developing for my clients all over the country.

You can also contact my office at **1-855-693-0699** with any questions you have, and I will be glad to help you implement these strategies for your business.

SECTION I

Fundamental Truths You Need To Believe

In this section, I am going to be laying down a foundation. There are lies you've been led to believe and truths that have been hidden from you. I'm hoping this section opens up your mind and gets you thinking differently. None of what I reveal to you is theory. This is experience and practice – years of testing and tweaking. You will need these truths to allow you to be successful trying any of the strategies I reveal to you later in this book.

CHAPTER 1

Your Revenue Problems Won't Be Solved By Trying To Get New Customers

Many small business owners believe that to generate more business, all they need are new customers. Salesmen push advertising to solve this, and it's true . . . to a point.

Every business needs an advertising strategy to bring in a stream of new customers. Remember, you have to keep bringing new customers in to make up for the people that you're losing through your leaky bucket. So you have to market for new customers, <u>but that should not be your only focus</u>.

The real revenue solution is getting repeat customers and getting them to spend more. Even with direct response marketing strategies that you'll learn from me, new customer acquisition always costs more. Based on my statistics, it costs you 5 to 10 times more to generate a new customer versus motivating and retaining current customers.

Think about how much money it costs you to acquire a new customer. Maybe you aren't tracking it closely right now, but you know how big that check is that you write to your ad rep each month, right? Very few businesses can rely on the same ad to produce a stream of customers week after week, month after month. You have to come up with new messages, new angles, and new offers to capture and keep attention. Every new ad you write needs to be bolder and bigger to outshine the competition. As response rates go down, you need to place more ads more frequently to keep up the stream of new customers.

Think about the advertising you do now. To get first-time customers, many businesses advertise loss leaders – highly discounted special offers to catch the eye and tempt the potential new customer. That means, most new customers you can get through the door aren't spending as much money with you in that initial visit, and you might be breaking even or losing money on that visit. What if they never come back? How long can you afford to lose money on every new customer and never have them walk back into your business?

In an ideal world, we want to generate a new customer *and* make profit on that initial transaction. Some of the strategies you'll learn here will do that, but maybe I'll be the first person to tell you this: **an intelligent business owner should be willing to lose money on the first transaction to get a customer in the door, but the REALLY intelligent owner has a strategy in place to get that customer to visit again, and keep them coming back again and again.** This is the customer stream we desire.

Do not waste the opportunity you have with a first time customer by failing to provide them fantastic service or a great product. That should be a given. But also take advantage of their attention. You and your staff should be up-selling and suggesting other services. You should be suggesting complimentary products and services to the one they are considering, or even offering more expensive versions of what they are interested in. Think about this as advertising within your four walls. You have their attention, so even producing brochures, posters, or videos to display at your business will take very little cost.

If you have to go through the cost and effort to get that customer BACK in the door using the same medium, you'll go out of business. It will always cost less to get your *existing* customers to return and get them to spend more while they are there, or soon after they buy. The difference all goes right to your bottom line.

Getting customers to spend more on each transaction can be as simple as "super sizing" or bundling services, perhaps as a special incentive for the month, or whatever period you decide. Ideas can be as simple as "Buy one get one half off" or offering a set amount off with an expenditure of a certain amount. Small revenue increments add up. For a restaurant owner who is serving 10,000 meals a month, an added profit of $1 per meal could bring in an additional $120,000 a year – with little additional overhead.

CHAPTER 2

You Will Never Be As Profitable As You Desire If You Fail To Track Advertising Results

Years ago I ran a restaurant and I was pretty much at the mercy of whatever marketing reps were offering me -- whether it was a radio sales rep or a phonebook ad rep. What drove me nuts was never knowing if I was getting my money's worth. They would never show me any way to figure it out. Now I know why - they'd sell fewer ads if I knew the awful response rates! I never knew I was overpaying to "reach" that mass number of people, most of whom I knew in my gut were never going to become a customer.

I am no longer a fan of placing ads without an offer that can be measured. I have to know how much revenue that ad produces for me or I will not run it.

The day I discovered Direct Response Advertising, I made myself a promise that I would only invest in 100% _trackable_ advertising.

Direct Response Advertising is a form of advertising whereby a prospect must take a specific action that is measurable. The better the offer to entice the action, the higher your response rate will be. Please visit **www.TheCustomerStream.com** to see examples of good Direct Response Advertising.

When you create an ad, these five elements must be included to get maximum response from your campaign. I learned these principles from my mentor, Dan Kennedy.

> 1. **Always include a reason for the ad**. Obviously, the person reading the ad knows you're selling something, but try to come up with a reason other than wanting the customer's money to run the ad! You want to offer a reason that's newsworthy, a big idea, or a valuable solution.

> 2. **You must include a headline that grabs the prospect's attention**. This big opening line calls out the reason for the ad. Its purpose is to get the person to stop everything else and read the ad.

3. **Don't put out weak offers**. You want the offer to be irresistible – so inviting that the prospect takes notice and wants to take action. Weak offers = Poor response. You'll see some strategies that present very strong offers in this book.

4. **Give the reader a reason to act NOW.** Not later. <u>Now</u>. Make sure the reason to act now is believable and compelling. Many ads will include a deadline – either a number or date where the offer is no longer valid.

5. **Tell the reader exactly what to do**. This is the *"Call To Action"*. If you want the person to call, clearly tell them to call and prominently display the phone number. If the action is to visit a website, tell them to visit, tell them why to visit, and prominently display the website address.

These are the elements you want to include in most direct response ads. There are others such as testimonials, guarantees and good ad copy, but these five elements above are critical.

The formula for determining the success of a Direct Response Ad is simple:

Gross Profit – Ad Spend = Net Profit

I will accept a loss on this transaction if I have a system in place to get some customers spending more on their first visit, or certainly if I have a system in place to increase the chances they return a second time (which by the way, you also can measure).

I personally like to do a lot of marketing through the mail. You'll see many of my strategies involve direct mail. Contrary to what you might believe, mail is not always more expensive than online strategies. I prefer to evaluate a strategy by its response and revenue, so I will never allow the cost of a campaign to deter me from making a decision alone. This is why I track campaigns. Don't be lured by the sexiness and cheap costs of online advertising and abandon everything else. You should be doing more of what works, online or offline. Honestly, I've found direct mail to work really well. It's actually good news for me and my clients that many people are too scared to try mail or mesmerized by the lure of online advertising alone.

Direct mail involves buying a list of people and mailing an offer. Then I actually know exactly (by name) who took me up on the offer and who did not. Did you ever consider how many people see your ad in the paper, in the phone book, or on that billboard and *didn't* come in? Wouldn't you love to know who didn't come in and have another shot at convincing them it's worth their time and money to come to you? Well, when you start off with a list of those you mail to, you know exactly who responded and who didn't. I use this information to keep in contact with the customers who came in and prepare a different offer for those that didn't.

You can see by targeting your likely prospects and tracking your response, you are much more in control of your marketing and cash flow. When I taught this principle to one of my clients, he told me that he feels he can almost generate revenue at will! I agree.

CHAPTER 3

Relying On Old School Marketing Methods Will Accelerate Your Decline

Let's look at closer traditional advertising mediums. Most local businesses have a presence in an advertising medium such as newspaper, radio or Yellow Pages. You feel you have to be in these types of media-- and that might be true, but there are some concerns.

For me, I cannot ignore the declining reach of certain media and the bias of certain media by demographic. For example, the Yellow Pages are still distributed, but how effective are they? Do you drag out the Yellow Pages when you need a plumber or a heating company, or want a pizza? No, you pull out your phone or go online. It's not wrong to place an ad in the Yellow Pages, but it is important to understand that generally speaking it only is going to be used by an older and less technologically sophisticated demographic. The phone book is a dying advertising medium and is not going to get you the response it once did.

As for newspapers, the days of people poring over the daily paper are over. Just read about the number of newspaper companies closing their doors, and the huge drop in ad rates in these publications. People just don't read the physical newspaper anymore, they go online to get their information and news. If you are placing ads in the newspaper, be aware that a large segment of the population won't be looking at it. Some people still get the weekend edition of their small local paper, but don't be fooled that just placing an ad here is going to solve your new customer acquisition problem.

What about radio? People still listen to the radio, but how do you know which radio station to advertise on? Everybody has a different taste in music, times of day that they listen to it, and how long they actually listen to it. So how do you know where and when to advertise? The advent of personal MP3 players has cut deeply into this medium, once again affecting the number of people you can reach effectively.

You have the same problem with TV advertising, and unless you have a type of product or service where you can get them to call in and respond immediately, you have no way of knowing if your expensive TV advertising is paying for itself. With the advent of cable and the Internet, people have more choices and channels to watch. This further fragments the audience and dwindles your chances of reaching many people at one time.

Furthermore, all of these media are dwindling in terms of the highly-favored demographics that most businesses are looking for – young adults with disposable income. If you work with an older population, these mediums may still be an option, but as time goes by the effectiveness of advertising in traditional media is going down.

Today you need strategies which are <u>unique</u>, which are <u>fun</u>, which are all <u>measurable,</u> and are <u>proven</u> to actually get customers streaming in the door and coming back.

CHAPTER 4

There Is No Such Thing
As A "Loyal Customer"

Some owners feel they don't have to worry about going out and getting new customers. "I have all the business that I can handle right now, and I have <u>a loyal customer base</u>" one told me.

This is ignorance at best, because every business is losing customers every day. A customer's circumstances change. They may get married or divorced, employed or unemployed. They move. According to the US postal service, about 18-26% of the population is moving at any given time. These and dozens of other factors can result in as much as a 50% customer loss per year.

There are those with established businesses that think: "I've been here for 35 years, people know where I am." They just make the assumption that everybody in town knows where they're located, knows what their business is, and knows what they offer, so further advertising isn't needed.

This again is marketing by hope. Hoping your customers remember you, hoping they know you provide X, hoping they need X, hoping they choose to drive to your location when a newer one just opened close by, and hoping that they will continue to pay your price when better pricing options are available at your competitor. This is foolish thinking to take your existing customers for granted. To stay in business you have to consistently give them reasons to keep doing business with you.

If you don't stay in touch with your customers they will forget about you, period. Unless you are the only restaurant in town, the only plumber, or the only jeweler, they have choices. This is a mobile society.

The "loyalty" of your customer will be tested by a competitor who puts a better offer in front of them. It is easy for somebody to just drive somewhere else to shop for those same services. If "your customer" has a good experience at that new competitor, you just might have lost them.

As hard as it is to gain a customer, it's much easier to lose one.

Businesses I'm involved with focus heavily on creating ways to keep in touch with people from the very first time they walk through the door, even before they buy anything. We make sure to collect as much information about each person as we can. That includes name, address, e-mail, phone, and other pertinent information. Of course, you aren't going to just get all of this information easily. Most people value their time and privacy so you have to be creative.

Why not have a drawing for a prize that requires their information to contact them if they win? You've all seen the fish bowl of business cards at the lunch place with a "Free lunch" pulled weekly from all the cards in the bowl (but how many of these places actually take the time to contact the people that didn't win?).

People will often give you some information if you promise to keep them updated with news and specials about your business, especially if they have a chance at winning something or getting a good deal. Customers will join a rewards or loyalty strategy to get special privileges and rewards for frequent visits or purchases, and you can require them to provide you with all kinds of good information in return.

All of the people that give you their information will form your "House List". Much of what I do strategically is based on the goal of growing the House List. The deeper and more accurate your house list, the better chance your business will have to survive and thrive. Use a database or some other electronic means to store this information so you can easily access it, sort it and use it.

CHAPTER 5

Know Your Customer – The Entire World Is Not Your Prospect

I can often trip up a business owner by asking him or her who the ideal customer is for their business. If the answer to my question is, "I don't know" or "Anyone" I know they are in trouble. I haven't met a small business owner on a budget that has the resources to reach and serve "Everyone."

Don't make the mistake of believing the whole world is your oyster when it comes to customers. You cannot afford to reach everyone, nor should you assume everyone is a perfect fit for what you offer. There aren't many businesses that service everyone in a community any longer. There are always choices for people, so why not help your new customers make a good choice by clearly demonstrating your ability to understand them?

It pays to think about what clientele you want to attract. Things like location, ages, gender, interest, culture, taste, design – everything you put out there has the ability to both attract and repel potential customers. People at different stages of life – young, older, single, family-oriented and so on – they all have different habits and like different things. For instance, if you own a pub, do you attract the college-age crowd or the blue collar crowd, professionals or sports fanatics? They can overlap, but it's really important for you to understand who makes up your demographic.

This can even involve the layout or décor of your office. You need to think long and hard about who is coming into your place, and who you REALLY want coming into your place. Believe it or not, you will affect the amount of money you make per customer by selecting the perfect profile to attract. Think about their expectations. Think about yours. You really have to know who you are and who you want to attract and then target that population. It's not just "everyone."

We now live in an age where we have more than two kinds of places to get your hair cut, not just a beauty parlor or barber shop. There are no-frill shops where you get a cut for less than ten dollars, high-end shops that cater to the affluent, sports themed salons for men, and salons for children and families. We have dentists that specialize in children's dentistry, dentists who focus on pain-free procedures, dentists with grand piano's and massage tables in the lobby, and dentists at your local super-store. There are car care service providers that specialize in brakes and mufflers, some in transmissions, some on just oil changes, some cater to women, and some that provide concierge service for busy professionals.

Your results will be better – and measurable – when you really take time to distinctly decide who your perfect customer is. You can focus your advertising which will save you money and increase response. You can sometimes charge higher fees when you can provide more specific experiences. You'll have an easier time staving off competitors when you carve a niche into a market and work hard at maintaining a solid customer base.

CHAPTER 6

Focus On The Lifetime Value Of Your Customer

Most businesses would benefit from implementing any one direct response marketing strategy, but they hesitate to implement anything despite proven results. Perhaps they think it won't fit in their advertising budget. I say, it's costing them more to NOT implement these strategies.

The key is knowing what a customer is worth to you. Let's look at some number scenarios.

If somebody spends $30 with you and they do that three times a month, that's $90. If they do that over the course of a year, it's over $1,000, and over three years it's over $3,000. Let's say it costs $4-5 dollars to send them a letter or post card and then you gave them a free entrée as part of that. You will also include them in a couple of later promotions. In relation to the $3,000 that customer is worth to you over 3 years, aren't you willing to absorb 10 to 15 dollars to get them in?

Keep things in perspective when figuring out what a customer is really worth to you. If you're in the auto repair business, you know customers should have their oil changed every three thousand miles or perhaps 3-4 times a year, depending on how much they drive. They'll come in multiple times for service if you do a good job. It's not about the oil changes though, because you can never tell when somebody's car is going to break down, and it cost hundreds and thousands of dollars to get an automobile repaired. I just had a wheel bearing go out on my car last week and it cost me about $400 to replace that. Do you believe it's worth it to spend $40 to get $400 out of me? That's a pretty good return on investment.

Here's what Jim R, a happy Transmission & Auto Repair shop owner had to say,

> *"I am very pleased with your "new customer" acquisition program. New customers are important to the growth of my auto repair business.*
>
> *We have been averaging 5-6% response on your mailings. Our new customer average ticket equals over $560.00 over*

one year. That's over $100,000 in new
revenue per year. Thanks!"

What about higher frequency businesses? People come in every week or two to a dry cleaner, nail salon, or hair salon. Regular transactions, even small amounts, add up quickly. Even for businesses like medical practices patients provide repeat and referral business. If you can keep a customer for months and even years it makes the cost of marketing seem insignificant. Wise marketers think about how to bring good customers in and are not concerned about how much it is going to cost. They are aware of the lifetime value of their customer and they work to retain their patrons.

> *"The man who will use his skill and con-*
> *structive imagination to see how* _much_
> *he can give for a dollar, instead of how*
> _little_ *he can give for a dollar, is bound to*
> *succeed."* – (Henry Ford)

A lot of people don't consider this. You're only looking at the cost of the marketing versus the pay off. Is your mindset more like , "Can I afford to spend this on this ad this week?" or, "If I spend $1 on advertising this week, will it bring me $2, $3 or more dollars within the next week or month?" Don't pinch pennies or just look for short term profits. Realize, as tracking will show, that a customer generated by good marketing will come into your business many times a year for three or more years. If you understand this you'll see marketing in a new light. You will look differently at that person who walks in the door regardless of what they buy. That person could be worth thousands to you over time and you only had to spend a few dollars to get them there. You'll look at people walking in the door and think, "Hey, that guy is worth 1,000 bucks to me. That guy is worth another thousand." Won't it influence how you treat them?

You have to think of your marketing in terms of an investment and, like any investor, you want to be able to measure the results – the short and, especially, the long term value of your investment.

SECTION II

Strategies For Getting Customers Through The Door

Now it's time to get specific. I hope you read the previous section with an open mind, because if you essentially agree with me, you'll understand how powerful these strategies will be for you, and how they can specifically and dramatically increase the efficiency and response of your advertising.

Even if you don't agree with my assumptions in the previous section, I challenge you to try these strategies I am about to reveal to you and simply test the results for yourself. If it isn't at least as successful as anything you are currently doing, I'd be surprised because these strategies are proven. I've used them in my businesses and my clients have used them in theirs. You will find them innovative, fun and effective. They are genius in terms of their simplicity. Yes, these involve a little work, but if you are already reading this book I know you're ready to do something good for your business. I bet your competitors wouldn't bother putting forth the effort you are willing to.

Remember, all these strategies involve direct response marketing. This form of marketing yields the stats you will use to measure how well each stage or strategy is working. I think that you, like so many clients I have worked with, will find this is a very cost-effective method of marketing.

Don't forget: Once they come in the door, you need to keep track of their information for future connection!

CHAPTER 7

The Birthday Strategy

The strategy that I have found to have the highest response rate for the most businesses is what I call **The Birthday Strategy**. The Birthday Strategy can be adapted for most any business. All you need to do is create a special offer to honor a person's birthday. I've used this strategy to draw in new customers in dozens of businesses, and it has been a launching pad for other successful marketing strategies. I'm going to spend time discussing the mechanics of this strategy in depth as several parts of this strategy are also used in other strategies I'm going to reveal to you.

The first thing you need to obtain is a list. There are lists available that tell almost everything there is to know about someone. Did you know most of the information on your driver's license is publicly available except the license number? So it's very easy to get a list of people in your community and know when their birthday is. You won't get the actual day of their birthday, but you will get the month – and that's all we need.

A birthday can be a good springboard for marketing because, whether they're still counting or not, most people, deep down, enjoy celebrating their special occasion in one way or another. I feel strongly that advertising has to be personalized in some way to be successful. If you simply send someone a regular mail piece or run an advertisement in the paper, it will carry much less weight. You're touching someone's emotions by recognizing them personally -- and people want to be recognized. My clients love when customers walk in the door and say, "Wow, how did you know it was my birthday?" This creates a friendly atmosphere and the opportunity for a conversation with you!

These lists, believe it or not, are easy to obtain. They can be purchased from any list broker. Simply Google the term "list broker" and you'll see hundreds to choose from. One of the most well-known brokers that you can use is InfoUSA (www.InfoUSA.com or 800.321.0869). Another is Zapdata.com. When you contact them, you can specify the type of list you want to purchase, including what you need for this promotion – name, address, birth month, and a specific area around your business location. (*Please note birthday information is considered confidential so the list company may need to approve your sales letter before you get the list. All the letters I use have been approved by my list company.)*

As you might guess, this works especially well for restaurants. Everybody loves to go out to eat on their birthday. The strategy is to send a potential new customer an offer for a free dessert, free entrée, 2-for-1, etc. They can redeem this offer any time during their birthday month. They may have other plans on their actual birthday, but a high percentage of people will certainly find time to come to you during their month to celebrate if the offer is good. Can you see how much fun this is for you and your new customer? **It works *REALLY* well!**

Here is what client Mike M. had to say about the birthday strategy:

> *"There's so many positive things with it ... we track it, so the numbers don't lie... and we've had from 38% to 58% response rate. We've never had a marketing tool that worked for us like this one has. It's someone's birthday and they are happy to get something in the mail... and they bring it in and they bring in friends and family. The redemption rate on that is great. We were getting back 3*

and 4 dollars profit on every dollar we spent on the strategy."

"Some people get the birthday offer that may have never been in the restaurant before and, you know, it's our job to treat them right... And we'd see those faces come back... And some of them sent us thank you cards afterwards!"

"I tell you, that's real refreshing, to get a thank you card from a customer... To think they spent the time to sit down and write it and put a stamp on it... We've never had a thank you from a radio ad!"

And here is what client John, a Supper Club owner from Granite Falls, MN had to say about the birthday strategy:

"Thanks for the great business you have developed and shared with me. I need to tell you how much my business has benefitted over the last six months. You are doing a great job."

"I was doing cold birthday mailings on my own before meeting you and signing up with NEW Customers NOW. My percentage of redemption rate on my own was a dismal 6% and I was losing money

every month on the promotion. True, I was acquiring about 20 new customers per month, but at a cost of over $6 per customer! In addition I was spending hours printing, labeling and applying postage. With the New Customers Now everything is done for me and I can concentrate on running my business. I spend a couple of minutes each month uploading my current customer list, which you sort and eliminated double mailings to guests that are already in my database. This is great!"

"The best news is that acquisition of new customers now generates profit! Redemption rate is over 20% with new customers now which is OVER 3 TIMES what I was getting on my own. The average guest spends an average of over $30 in addition to the discount and generates a profit of over $9 for each card redeemed. This works out to about $1.68 for each card sent. This is as close to a money machine as it gets."

When is the last time you ever got a thank you card from your customer? As you can see, the response rates for this promotion can be high. The average returns for restaurants I normally see with The Birthday Strategy are between 20% and 50%. Bear in mind, we're not sending these offers to people who have frequented our business before. These are "cold" leads: we're contacting people who've never done business with us before, and may have never heard about us or expected to receive mail from us. So getting 20% of the recipients to walk into your business for the first time has to get you excited!

Now consider this: if 1,000 offers were sent out, figuring just a 20% response rate, that's 200 new people that will come into your business for that month. In a business like a restaurant, people usually don't go alone, and especially not for their birthday. They bring along family or friends. So you have a much higher probability of getting what is known in the restaurant business as a '4- topper', which is a fully-seated table (the National Restaurant Association estimates 2.8 to be the average for the number of people that go out to eat with a birthday celebrant). If you're looking to fill tables there is no better way than to send out a birthday greeting to get somebody to come into your restaurant and bring three or four people with them?

Perhaps you are thinking, how can this work for *MY* business? People aren't going to bring along three others when they get their car serviced or their teeth cleaned. True. Your offer and your response rate will be different, but your profit margins are likely to be higher than a restaurant, especially since there is a greater opportunity for additional products and services that you can offer them.

The Birthday Strategy, done right, can produce really exciting results. Like many business owners that have previously done any sort of tracking on their marketing, you know that getting even a 1% response rate on a mail piece is often considered a victory. To get 10%, you'd be jumping to the ceiling and high-fiving everyone around, but to get 20%, 30%, 40%, even 50% is completely unheard of for most businesses. This is a marketing strategy that's worth trying, wouldn't you say?

The Nitty-Gritty of the Birthday Strategy

There are certain components to this strategy you must carefully execute to make it effective. It's not just simply sending out a birthday card with an offer. There are some things you have to do -- and not do.

The mistake that a lot of business owners make is to trying to do everything on the cheap. They'll send out a little 4 X 6 postcard to acknowledge the person's birthday -- and they may get a fair response with that -- but that doesn't stand out. You want to send something that grabs the prospect's attention and sticks in their memory.

You want to send your greeting in an envelope. In itself, this is a risk, because when you're doing direct mail, the first hurdle you must jump is getting the envelope opened. The worst mistake you can make here is making it look like all the other junk mail you receive in an envelope.

The late Gary Halbert referred to an A pile and B pile. Everything that went into the A pile was mail you knew you were going to open -- bills or greeting cards or correspondence from acquaintances; important things you knew you were going to sit down and look at. The B pile is the disposable stuff that might be briefly looked at, or dropped immediately into the garbage can. Think about this for yourself – you dump most anything that looks like junk mail right into the trash.

To avoid landing in the "B" pile, I found these ideas work well:

"Handwrite" the person's address on the envelope (first and last name) so that it looks like somebody has spent the time to write a letter to them. You should actually handwrite the addresses yourself, have your staff do this, or hire out a printer that can do this. With a really good printing press, you can use a cursive font that mimics the real thing very well, or some printers also have people that perform this service (you can contact me at doug@thecustomerstream.com or **1-855-693-0699**. I have the ability to save you a lot of time on this step)

Use a blind return address – don't use a logo or business name up there – just use the street address in case it needs to be returned (because you want to track and remove undeliverable addresses from your list).

Stick on an actual live stamp. If you use any type of indicia, which is either machine applied or marked as presorted mail, that's easily identified as coming from a business. You should never use bulk mail. I know this sounds like a lot of effort, but there are printing companies like mine with specialized equipment that can automate most of this process. It's worth it for many businesses to outsource this to a printing company, especially if you are going to do this in volume, but that doesn't mean you can't do this yourself in small quantities on your own. Remember, the effort is worth it considering the terrific response rates you'll see with this strategy!

If you get the person to open the envelope, you've won a small battle. Your attention must now be to get the person to actually read what's inside.

Here's some time-tested tactics to get people to read your offer:

Get personal. Studies have proven that if the letter has the person's name in it, they have a low likelihood of throwing it away immediately. They're going to at least read it and find out what it's about. So use their name often.

Include a birthday letter and a birthday certificate, both of which are personalized to the recipient.

Mention their name often. There is research showing the different ways people read, and what areas of a letter the eye most frequently scans, so make sure to mention the recipient's name in a more than one place, but certainly beginning with the Happy Birthday _____ ! salutation.

Use persuasive sales copy. In separate paragraphs, explain that you are offering something special for their birthday and tout what's special about your business.

Make the person an irresistible offer that has few or no strings attached to it. The offer will vary by business, but for a restaurant it's usually a free entrée valued up to a certain dollar amount with no other stipulations on it (such as that somebody else has to come with them, or that they have to buy another one of equal or greater value). It's a generous offer that impresses prospects. Don't get cheap here because a weak offer has very little chance of generating a response.

Include a few short testimonials in your letter so that you give people some proof that other people have had a good experience with your business in the past.

The letter should be hand-signed. (Most of my clients have me emulate their signature and print that for them.)

Make the certificate valid for a month. You need to make sure to get it in the client's hands by the first of the month so they have a full 30-31 days to redeem the certificate. *The full name and address of the person should be on the certificate*, so that when it is redeemed, you can build a list of people who have demonstrated a willingness to do business with you (your House List). Print the offer on the certificate along with the date that it expires **boldly displayed**. On the back, list the hours of operation, your website, phone numbers, a map, and any pertinent information. You want to make sure the certificate leaves no doubt as to what you are offering, where they can find you, the hours and days you are open, and how to get to your business in case they throw away the letter and only keep the certificate. (You know --- the magnet on the refrigerator reminder.)

Where and Who You Send the Letter To Is Important

Before you consider purchasing a list of people try to target a demographic of the type of person that's a good fit for your business. It's not going to be cost-effective to mail everyone in a certain radius of your business. It will only lower your response rate and decrease the chances the offer turns a profit. When I am working with my clients on The Birthday Strategy we figure out factors like age, income, proximity to the place of business, whether the prospective customer is a home owner or not and other pertinent criteria. For instance, home ownership is important because people who live in apartments tend to be more transient, so you're going to have a higher percentage of undeliverable mail to these folks.

You need to determine all the factors that best identify your likely client for your business.

Depending on whether you're in a rural or a metropolitan area, you can determine how far out you can expect people to respond. Rural residents expect to drive a distance to get to any business. If you're in a metropolitan area, there are a lot of choices that are available to people. They are used to shopping more locally. Consider these things as you decide how wide an area the mailing should cover. If you're in a brick and mortar business and want a customer to visit your location, don't waste your marketing dollars paying to go outside your area. You want to control who's actually seeing your ad so that you reach a likely customer.

Always look for "the highest probability customer." This might not be something you can easily do without a lot of experience. Frankly, a valuable part of the services my company provides (besides the busy work of actually putting together these mailings) is helping you select the demographic that will most likely yield the highest response rate and those customers that are likely to spend money with you on a regular basis.

Making the Birthday Strategy Work for Your Non-Restaurant Business

Obviously the birthday promotion works very well for restaurants but other businesses can use this strategy to generate customers and still get great results. You just need to think creatively and tweak the strategy to fit your business.

Auto repair is a good niche to use this strategy. In this type of business, not everybody needs the work done at a given time. Someone's need for maintenance work or auto repair, or to get his or her oil changed, may not land within the birthday month so you will generally find that the percentage of redemptions is lower; however, the average *transaction* within an auto repair shop is significantly higher than it is in a restaurant. Therefore, it allows you to economically bring in new customers because there's always a certain number who are ready to have some automotive work done or have their oil changed. For this reason you could choose to lengthen the redemption period.

The same factors apply for nail salons, hair salons, clothiers, chiropractors, dentists, etc. Be creative – you can offer a free pedicure for someone's birthday, a free trim or color touchup, free accessory, free adjustment, free massage, free cleaning, or free visit.

Offering a free service will likely reveal some other work or service that can be added on so you have a great chance of follow-up business immediately.

Any local business, if you're creative enough, can think of something to give away via the birthday certificate to entice a first-time customer. You just need to make sure you understand it's not just what you are interested in giving out. It has to be what the consumer is interested in receiving. Your focus should be "What can I offer a customer that they will want? How can I make this a win-win promotion?"

The Birthday Strategy is 100% trackable. You can track the results of every mailing to see if you have a great promotional offer or not. To improve response on the next mailing, you can try different options, different offers, or different specials. You can test something new each month and compare those results to other months. When you find a winner, run with that offer a few months before you test another offer.

Don't be the business owner who mails out 100 of these offers, gets a poor response, and says "I tried direct mail, it didn't work." You must be committed to this and be very honest in evaluating your efforts. This strategy will cost more than mailing a coupon or postcard. Remember, if you cut corners, or put out a weak offer, you cannot expect a miracle. Hope, as you now know by now, is not a marketing strategy I want you to use any longer.

I've laid out the strategy for you here and you can see the actual pieces I use at **www.TheCustomerStream.com**. If you have the ability to hire someone to do this or need my advice please don't hesitate to contact me at **1-855-693-0699**. Take advantage of my experience. I've spent years testing and figuring out what works. This book and my experience are ways you can shave off a lot of time and aggravation -- and save a lot of money.

CHAPTER 8

The Belated Greetings Strategy

With The Birthday Strategy, we expect to get a good (or great) response nearing 20% - 50%, but that means at least 50% - 80% decided not to take our offer. Out loud we wonder, "How could *anyone* not love this offer I sent them?" True. The offer you sent was probably fantastic, but there are always reasons why people won't respond to an offer. In many cases it's nothing wrong with the offer at all, it could simply be they were preoccupied or busy.

For **The Belated Greetings Strategy** to work you will need to heed my instructions in the previous strategy. You must have printed the name and address of every recipient on the birthday certificate. This tells you who responded, and who did not. This strategy will blow your mind, and also blow the mind of your future customer. This strategy calls for you to send them a belated birthday card saying, *"We're sorry that you couldn't come in."*

How is that for genius? The person reading this card realizes that you're aware that they didn't come in. This shows them you're paying attention, and all of a sudden, you're standing out from every other business they frequent – just because you can tell whether they responded to your birthday offer or not.

Ask almost any business owner when somebody came in last – even regular customers -- they probably don't have a clue. By tracking The Birthday Strategy campaign, you know with certainty who didn't come in to celebrate their birthday. Your follow-up card is offering them a second chance to come in. This innovative strategy is another tool in generating a stream of customers. The response rates on this belated birthday strategy are usually less than the original but it's still a 10, 20, or 30% response rate.

This time you send out an oversized postcard (measuring 5.5" x 11") which is less expensive than sending out a full letter and certificate. You aren't spending as much to have a second chance to put your name before them, so a lower response rate is acceptable. A card of this size doesn't cost much more for printing and production than a normal 4x6 postcard, and it gets more attention in the mail than a small postcard. The big postcards you send should be high quality, and full color. People will notice them in their stack of mail and won't throw them away without reading them. You can see examples of a Belated Greeting postcard at **www.TheCustomerStream.com**.

I always try to add a picture on the card that catches their attention. These images are stock photos that you can obtain on a site like www.istockphoto.com, or you could simply have a family member or friend help you with "a model." The picture I love to use is of a baby crying – and, of course, the baby's crying "because you didn't come in." Whether the prospect sees the sadness or the humor, it's another way to engage an emotion – always a good marketing strategy. You can choose any number of stock photos but whenever you can, use a picture that is meaningful to your business. You can use somebody that works at the business, a child or grandchild, or maybe your dog. Use a cute photo that people will talk about. You want customers to come in and ask, "Whose baby is that?" or "Whose dog is that?" It helps further develop a relationship between you and your customers.

Your marketing pieces should strive to become conversation starters -- and not just for you and your employees. You want your prospect to be picking up the mail, see your postcard, and stop to show the neighbor across the street. That's free to you and leads to another potential customer. Get people talking. Don't be boring!

CHAPTER 9

The New Mover Strategy

Anyone who's moved knows that within a week or two of moving in you get a big bag of coupons on your door as part of some local new mover campaign. Businesses are persuaded to advertise through these welcome-to-the-neighborhood programs. The new neighbor gets inundated with all kinds of offers from dozens of service providers in the area. This strategy works for the right type of business: the dry cleaner, maybe the florist, perhaps an offer from the cable company, and certainly coupons from the pizza places and fast food joints because no one feels like cooking after a move. As time passes though, this packet gets lost in a drawer or tossed in the trash. If you don't get a customer's attention within the first couple days, you likely lost the opportunity with that program.

The New Mover Strategy I'm going to offer you a different way to advertise to new movers.

The Birthday Strategy provides an effective model to use here. You want to use a handwritten envelope, a blind return address, and a real postage stamp – but we wait to send this, because they've just moved and they're still getting oriented. Don't send the new mover campaign out the first month they move in. In fact, wait until 4-5 months after they've arrived. Think about it, when somebody's just moved in, they're busy and easily distracted. They're putting their things away, they're getting organized, and if they get anything in the mail, they might take notice of offers that will fit into what they need at the moment – fast food, lawn care, groceries, or dry cleaners. Wait a few months before you send them a letter.

A huge advantage to sending a letter rather than including a flyer in a door hanger is that the mailing is from your business alone. You're not competing for attention with coupons from fifty other businesses that are in the area. You're the only one who is offering them something at this time. When you create an offer, you know it will stand out.

All the same great offers that you came up with on The Birthday Strategy will work here too. Expect this strategy to have a lower response than The Birthday Strategy. I've discovered that movers often take a little more effort. This first letter you send may not get more than 10-20% to respond. Of course, as with The Birthday Strategy, you have their name and address on the certificate so you can keep tabs on who comes in and follow up with the no-shows.

Due to the lower response rates, you need to get innovative. If you take a look at the mailing pieces for this strategy at **www.TheCustomerStream.com** you will see a handwritten letter that's on yellow legal paper and a letter that looks like it's been written by a child in crayon. You can choose to model either of these and I guarantee it's going to make you stand out. The person reading this letter is going to wonder whose child wrote this. Again, the offer may be the same as before, but this second letter has a touch of humor and makes you seem more approachable.

This kind of off-beat mailing usually brings a good response. Again, we always follow-up with the non-responders: next you send out an oversized postcard, perhaps featuring a cute little girl that's looking for someone and text that says, "Where are you? We know that you just moved into the area. We're looking for you. Please come in. Here's (whatever the offer is) to entice you to visit." You should attempt to reach out to them up to three times to get them in the door.

Obviously, those who don't respond to the first offer get a second, and those that don't respond to the second offer get a third. You always narrow the list down. Plan to do the strategy over a three-month period, so once a month you send them something different. It's the same offer but the mail piece is different. Unexpected events may affect turnout at any stage but with this strategy – or any of these strategies -- you have a fun back-up ready.

CHAPTER 10

The Mystery Shopper Strategy

So far, I've described strategies that utilize a purchased or 'cold' list as a starter. In each case your aim should be to keep track of who responds and use that data to build a house list of customers.

This next strategy can be done using a cold list or your house list. **The Mystery Shopper Strategy** involves sending out a short survey and asking the recipient to come in and secretly shop your business in order to find out how good your customer's experience is. As an owner, you need to know the experiences of your customers – to see where you excel, and where you need to make improvements. Any negative experience (perceived or real) by your customers has a direct effect on whether they will return and recommend you to their friends and family. By discovering things you are doing right you can highlight those things in your marketing. As a bonus, some of the surveys turn into customer testimonials.

To facilitate mystery shopping we send the patrons a letter explaining that we'd like them to come in to our place of business. It states: "We'd like you come in and partake of our service (in some way) and here is a survey we'd like you to fill out to tell us how we did. Please don't fill out the survey while you're here; we want you to complete it after you go home. Then send the survey back to us. We want your purpose and identity to be a secret or a mystery while you are in our business so that there will be no special efforts by any staff to influence you."

In order to get this level of cooperation you will have to give customers a reward for **completing the survey**. Just like the other strategies, your offer must be enticing in order to get the action you desire. You can offer discounts, free service, or even offer payment or a bonus to mystery shoppers. You cannot offer the customer any incentive to "shop" you the first time because if they turn in any sort of certificate or coupon they will blow their cover. That's not what we desire. So the nice thing about this strategy is it not only provides you valuable information on how you're doing with customers, it also gets people in your door two times. They come in and maybe they pay for themselves or a companion the first time and then they come back in a second time to cash in the offer you sent them for returning the survey.

You will find the components of an example Mystery Shopper Strategy at **www.TheCustomerStream.com.**

CHAPTER 11

The No Peeking Strategy

Many businesses experience slow periods. It may be tied to the weather, the seasonal calendar, school schedules or holiday activities. For whatever reason, people are just not coming in. **The No Peeking Strategy** is geared toward improving the customer stream during the slow periods. This strategy is designed to get people out of the house and into your business.

For example, there are certain parts of the country where towns empty out during the summer and everybody goes to the lake. On the other hand, in a lake town everybody comes in on the weekends and they are slower during the week. Most businesses know historically when their slow time is. I am sure there are certain months and certain local situations that your business faces where you could profit from The No Peeking Strategy.

This strategy is like a game and everyone is a potential winner. To get started you print up letters or certificates offering a set of prizes and seal them in envelopes marked "No Peeking!" These prizes are guaranteed to be given out, and each certificate is good for some sort of reward. These are handed out ahead of the expected slow time to people who come into your business. To receive their prize, customers must bring the envelope back in, unopened, to find out what it is.

To get a really clear idea of what this looks like head over to the website **www.TheCustomerStream.com** to see a couple examples of No Peeking Envelopes & Certificates I've used for my clients.

You should gear this strategy to your need. For instance, if you know that the first two months of the year are to be slow, hand out the envelopes during November and December for redemption in January and February. I have clients who do this two or three times a year! Every business is different. This strategy capitalizes on the customer stream that you already have coming into your place of business during the busy time and incentivizes customers to return during a slower time when they otherwise might not visit.

CHAPTER 12

The Turning Lemons
Into Lemonade Strategy

Hoping people will overcome all the obstacles to do business with you is not a marketing strategy! The "Lemonade" strategy originally was created to solve a problem one of my clients was having.

I received a call from an owner who had road construction going on in front of his restaurant. It's a nightmare for any business to have road crews working out front. With all those orange cones and barricades, equipment and activity, it is often too intimidating for customers to attempt to get in. Worse yet, he was on a highway just out of town. Even though the construction company kept his driveway open and accessible during the entire time, people were not coming in to eat because it looked like a hassle. His customer stream dropped off significantly and he needed help. Then I created **The Turning Lemons Into Lemonade Strategy**.

First, I went out there and took a few pictures of the owners beside some of the road equipment. I made them wear the orange vests and the hard hats and everything, and I had them acting like they were pulling their hair out. I took a few photos and printed them up on a large postcard with a headline that said, *"This Road Construction is Driving Us Crazy."*

There is a picture of the card at **www.TheCustomerStream.com**

We mailed these postcards to people all around town. We figured that we may not get the drivers off the highway but we can get the locals in here if we make sure they know we're still open for business and that the entrance is accessible.

We sent this out a few times during the months of the road construction, adding twists like a countdown of days until the road crews would be finished, and we got 25% to 33% redemption on those oversized postcards!

Think these are incredible response rates? Here is what that construction-blocked restaurateur says:

"I've been with Doug for a couple of years now. We started when we had the unfortunate thing of having road construction right in front of our restaurant. We did a fun promotion, with myself and my business partner holding up signs. And we sent out these cards, with an odd offer... it was a 5 dollar and 9 cents offer. People got a kick out of it. We looked pretty silly, and the odd offer got them talking. People came in and asked us, "Why $5.09?" It was pretty effective. We got good redemption rates. As I recall, we had 25% the first month, 29% the second and 33% the third."

"Any time you can track something like that, the proof is in the pudding, so to speak. The numbers don't lie, you send so many out and you get so many back. (We sent out this fun piece) and pretty soon people were waiting to be seated. The five dollar and nine cent offer was unique. People talked about that. I know they won't forget that odd amount."

That promotion is something that will linger in his customers' memory for a while. People will remember his restaurant.

The question for you is, how can you apply this to your business? Are you a retailer with a big box store that moved in across the street? Instead of crying in your coffee, how about turning the situation around and show yourself in front of your new competitor and coming up with a creative picture? What if you had a hail storm damage your inventory? What about a heat wave or cold spell that kept people indoors and away from your business?

The formula is simple: take that ugly situation that's keeping customers away, find a way to interject some humor, then create an offer and mail it out to people close to your business. Remember, doing nothing is hope. Now you know you can turn obstacles into a winning marketing strategy!

CHAPTER 13

The Internet Strategy

Odds are, you have a website, and you have tried some form of internet advertising. As you may have already experienced, generating new customers online isn't so easy. To talk about all the nuances and things you should be doing online would take an entire book. What I intend to do here is give you several things which I feel are important regarding your **Internet Strategy**.

First, in terms of search engines, don't fall for the trap of people selling you on "registering" your business with 100 search engines. It's a lie. There are only three search engines you need to consider, because together, 99% of all web searches happen through them.

Google, Yahoo, and Bing (Microsoft) are the only engines you need to consider. Getting your website "registered" with these three giants is very easy.

For Google, go to **www.google.com/places**

For Bing, go to **www.bing.com/businessportal**

For Yahoo, go to **listings.local.yahoo.com**

They've made this extremely simple for business owners to complete on their own. All you need to do is follow the prompts. Fill out basic information about your business, including links to your website. Best of all, these services are provided for free. You are actually losing money by not "claiming your listing" on all three of these search engines.

Next, about your website, make sure you give people information that they want. Your website is probably not going to be set up to take orders for your products online. That's not to say you cannot sell something from your website, but your real aim is to get these viewers to physically come into your brick and mortar place of business.

Make it look attractive – photos, graphics, and easy to read layout are important. Make it interesting. There are generic websites available, where you just add your name, rank and serial number, what the business is or does, location and hours of business, and maybe an interactive Contact Us page. The fault, to my mind, is that there is no personal touch there. I suggest you add a video, where you are talking to the customers, communicating what you want people to know about you and your business. You can use the camera to show them your place and bring out certain points that are special about what you offer.

Your website should be an opportunity to introduce services that the public isn't aware that you have – and that they may need. Let's say you provide services as a dentist. There are a lot of people out there that aren't aware of all of the problems that you can treat or what kind of up-to-the minute equipment you may use. People may be intimidated or missing health benefits because of their misconceptions about your services.

In you are a chiropractor, many people may think you only help people with a bad back or a neck that's kinked. Tell them that you treat sore knees and ankles too. Talk about how you treat problem areas. Do you use acupuncture or other treatments? With a video presentation, you can reduce a lot of the fears that a person may have and overcome their reluctance to come in for a consultation.

You are able to develop a relationship with the customers more easily through video because they hear you talking to them and they feel they have a connection with you. But video or not, you should be offering information through your website – and asking prospects for their name and e-mail address for it. Use your website to gather contact information about prospective customers and build your House List. Offer something valuable that the visitor must fill in some personal information to receive. It might be a discount coupon to be sent to their e-mail. It could be an informative brochure or booklet to be mailed to their home. It could even be an invitation to join your Birthday Club! Add these prospects to your database, and follow up with offers.

You have to incorporate online strategies with offline strategies for the maximum response. Once a customer comes in, you will collect additional information to use for other strategies. The internet may be tricky for generating new customers for local brick-and-mortar businesses but you can definitely use it for getting them back in again and again. You can keep in contact with them through e-mail with informative messages, discount offers, or maintenance appointment reminders. For example, a forward-thinking auto shop owner can use his House List to alert customers of new services or add a snippet to raise awareness that there are various things that need to be serviced on a vehicle.

Please be aware that sending out mass mailings electronically can be interpreted as spam. Not only will they get caught in the individual's spam filters, major service providers have been known to blacklist spammers which means your email won't get to your intended recipients at all.

However, if a customer has signed up with you and given you their e-mail contact information, you can make little videos and send these out to customers periodically so they can see you talking about a new approach or service. Some business owners send out a short newsletter periodically, either by regular mail or e-mail. You also can keep customers interested with news they can use about your specific business or the industry in general and fun things like trivia.

Lastly, if yours is the type of business where a customer is out and about, and might suddenly have need of your business, then you certainly must consider mobile marketing. There's been a lot of hype in the media about mobile marketing, and it's still a growing industry. Understand that as more consumers are getting smart phones with internet capability it is already showing a potential for taking over laptops and desktops as a person's main means of computing and communicating. So people will increasingly use their phones for Internet and e-mail. It would be a wise move to consider how your website looks on a mobile device and whether someone searching on their phone can find you and get to your website.

Google has made some tools available free for business owners to get mobile. Just check your Google Places account or contact a local web designer who is capable of assessing your needs for a mobile website and can build you one inexpensively. These websites need to be extremely efficient with information, low on fancy graphics and text. They are designed to give only the most pertinent information and a means to direct the customer to your place of business. You do not need a mobile site with more information than that. Make sure you are aware of new advances like this and see how you can take advantage of them to get new customers into your business, or get current ones to return.

CHAPTER 14

The Daily Deal Strategy

Daily Discount Deals are a relatively new phenomenon that everyone is talking about. Groupon and Living Social are the dominant players, and many other companies and businesses are employing some sort of **Daily Deal Strategy**. These deals leverage social media within a city to get a critical mass of people to "take the deal" before the discount or deal takes effect.

These offers have the potential of streaming a significant amount of new customers into your business at one time. You may have thought about trying it to boost your business and it might be a great strategy for you, but beware that it also can be a potential nightmare.

Why? These deals work because consumers love them. Discounts are eye-catching. We're not talking about small discounts, we're talking 50-90% off types of deals. In fact, these are the type of offers I teach you to put out because it can generate a lot of response.

In addition, the number of deals getting pushed to a customer's e-mail or mobile phone is staggering. The potential exists for it to produce a lot of activity for your business, and bring an exciting stream of customers during the offer's redemption period that may have never heard of you or stepped through your doors before.

You will definitely see a stream of new business with this type of strategy, but is this the holy grail like these companies claim? There's always a gotcha, and I want you to be informed.

> **Warning #1 -** If you don't have a system in place to track who's coming in and capturing their information, it's only going to be a one shot deal. Those deal-seekers are going to come in and try you, but they may or may not come back, especially if you're living in an area where there's a lot of competition.

> Remember, there's a new deal being promoted every day. The deal seekers are getting new experiences all the time. You have to give them a memorable experience when they come to you or they may not return. If you haven't captured their names you have no way to invite them back.

Warning #2 - Be aware that this method of new customer acquisition comes at a very high cost. You can't make money with everybody walking into your establishment with an 80% discount certificate or a coupon in their hand for your products and services. If these people are only deal seekers they are only looking for cheap deals and will never come back.

Warning #3 - Read the fine print. Some of these daily deal companies have very stringent rules about what you can offer. Like I said, it has to be an over-the-top deal. 60, 70, or 80% discounts are common and a majority of the money you collect goes directly to the daily deal company. You better have a system in place to build repeat business and get revenue from their return visits. Unfortunately many businesses are going to be very disappointed with their overall results because they weren't prepared to make these deals work effectively for them.

You have to have the mindset, "If I can break even or better on this, then I'm ahead of the game. I'll get all these new customers almost immediately, but I also need to put in place the systems to capture the data so I can get a return on my investment going forward." That's how you should be looking at it.

You need to be tracking every marketing method, and this is just another marketing method. Be thinking how can you turn this around and make it profitable in the long run. I personally know two businesses had to close because very few customers came in after that super discount was over. They lost a lot of money.

I'm suggesting you consider this as a strategy against other ones and weigh the pros and cons. Make a decision based on the return on your marketing dollars and the potential for it to produce customers that come back to you time and time again. No strategy you will ever employ is without risk. Your job is to always weigh risk and reward and invest your marketing dollars wisely.

CHAPTER 15

The Coupon and Valpak Strategy

You've probably advertised in a medium like the Happenings Book, Valpak, The Entertainment Book, or something similar. **The Coupon and Valpak Strategy** can bring in new customers, but I have some suggestions that will increase the likelihood they it will be successful for you.

In my own experience, these mediums bring people in to your business but they often bring people in from outside of your marketing area, which is a drawback. There's not a high likelihood that you're going to get that person back in again if the driving distance is significant.

With a cooperative mail service like Valpak, you can control thing a little bit more because you can segment the area that you're sending it to and make sure it is close enough for a likely response. The drawback is that inside of that envelope you are competing with 25 or more local businesses for attention -- and some of those are your direct competitors. The packet may not get opened. You may or may not get seen. As sexist as it sounds, a lot of men just don't care about couponing, so they throw it out. Their wives may be more likely to open it and pull out the coupons they think they're going to use, but it's often a quick sort, the rest are tossed, and you can only hope yours is chosen and used before it expires. Review the five principles of Direct Response Marketing I shared earlier in the book to increase the likelihood you will get the response you need. *This is in Section I - Chapter 2 – You Will Never Be as Profitable as You Desire If You Fail to Track Advertising Results.*

With Valpak, you are spending a certain amount to get in front of a large number of people. Your costs tend to be low per possible viewer but the response percentage also is usually very low. Most of these cooperative mail strategies send out to about 10,000 homes in a market area but you may only see 0.1% to 1.0% redemption of your coupons. The competition for attention in the stack and other factors such as the disparity of households in a zip code area affect the response rate. You are quite possibly marketing to people who can't afford to be your client. You can't target who you're going after like you can when you purchase a list, like breaking it down by age, income or household. Valpak and similar strategies may seem inexpensive but it's shotgun marketing rather than demographic marketing.

If yours is a brand new business and you don't yet have a very good idea who your most lucrative target market is, something like Valpak may be a good way to inexpensively introduce yourself to 10,000 homes. As long as you have a system in place to capture the information of those who come in your establishment you can keep marketing to them. This strategy will help you begin to grow your business.

SECTION III

Strategies For Getting Customers To Come Back In And Spend More

We have already discussed the fallacy of focusing all your efforts on new customer acquisition. While you need a system for bringing in new customers, constantly doing business by giving away or heavily discounting your services defeats your purpose, which presumably is to *stay* in business and be profitable.

In these next chapters, I'll share ways you can turn your new customer streams into repeat customer streams.

CHAPTER 16

The House List Strategy

In most of the strategies I have described so far, I have referred to building **The House List**. I often start off a new customer acquisition strategy by *purchasing* a list. I also call this a 'cold' list - basically a list of strangers. The House List is much different. I refer to it as a 'warm" list because it is filled with the names and addresses of those who are no longer strangers to your business. They have come in, made transactions, and become your customers.

This is actually *the biggest asset* you have: a list of customers who have demonstrated an interest and a willingness to do business with you. Build it. Guard it. Use it. The House List is a gold deposit waiting to be mined and can be a real moneymaker for you.

Who pays for the building around you, the equipment in there, and the employees walking in and out of there every day? It's your customers -- your most important asset, coming in and spending money with you.

If you run a business such as a restaurant or a nail salon you want to have your seats full. If you own an auto repair shop you want to have all your bays full with a line of other vehicles waiting to come in when one empties out. If you own a medical or dental practice, you want a full appointment schedule. Having a customer list is very, very valuable because you can use it to generate money. With this list, you have a direct connection to proven customers. You can contact them any time you choose. You can keep in touch. You can construct offers that will bring them back in the door.

> **The whole idea behind the house list is that *it gives you a source of revenue that you can tap at will*. You choose the marketing and the timing to suit your needs.**

There are a number of ways to build your House List. In the strategies that I have described -- The Birthday Strategy and The New Movers Strategy, for example -- the certificates that they bring in have their name and address. Remember how I stressed this? You could keep those in a file drawer, and it's not impossible to do some of this on paper, but you will more likely start a computer database, using Excel or some other software.

The more information you can get from the customer, the more valuable your list, because you have more ways to reach your customers. These days you're foolish if you're not collecting e-mail addresses. A phone number is important, especially a mobile phone number, because you can send them a text message. People usually read their texts before they read their e-mail, although many can access both from their smart phones. Technology allows you to do certain things less expensively. Contact via the e-mail is one option. There are also services that you can use to do an automated broadcast of information to their home phone or answering machine to announce a special event that's coming to your place of business. You'll want to let them know ahead that you may do this. Direct contact is significantly cheaper and has a much better response than if you just put a big ad in the paper. You should know this by now! You should try and collect birthdays, for obvious reasons. You want to be able to get customers back into the business by using a birthday as a reason for contacting them.

How do you get this detailed information? You can, of course, ask for it directly, or you can set up in-house strategies or promotions to entice customers to provide it. You can provide a small form at the check-out desk or in the waiting room, with a sign urging customers to fill out the information in order to participate in exchange for a reward or enticement. You might try a drawing, or an offer in connection with an event. I'm certain you can find an incentive to get them to give you their contact information. Funny enough, if you have a form set out, people will often sign it automatically, assuming that they're going to get something from you going forward. Holding a drawing gives you a valid reason to be collecting information, so that if they win, you can contact them by e-mail, you can mail them, or you can phone them. All of that makes sense to the customer and they're much more willing to give up their information. After all, they *want* to be contacted if they are the winner of the prize or prizes that you're setting up in your promotion.

You will want to test ideas to see what works and you may have to give different incentives, but you have to think about ways to collect as much of that information as you can. (I discuss some more ideas at the end of the book.)

With any promotion you do, including online advertising, you should be thinking of how to build your House List -- by offering something informational or a notification of 'specials', for example -- something that they have to contact you to obtain. Customers will give you their preferred forms of contact. For instance, some don't like giving out their cell phone number to people other than immediate family, others may give you their land line. Everybody has information that they are willing to give out or not.

A word of caution: I know business owners who think the only piece of information they want to collect is the e-mail address. Why? Because they think that's a free way they can contact large numbers of customers and stay in touch with them. That is a mistake because the rate of people reading e-mails is shrinking. Everybody is getting inundated with way more electronic mail than he or she can keep up with. Spam filters can take your message straight into the junk file. Relying on "a free way to contact them" can end up being a huge mistake. Stats are showing that only about 10 percent of all e-mails you send are being received and opened. So while e-mail is technically "free", it can be very costly and only reach 10% of your list at a time because an undelivered or unread marketing message earns nothing for you.

Your customers are valuable. If you do good marketing what difference does it make if it costs you money to contact somebody, if you know that you're getting that money back, plus some?

What's that old saying -- "Spend a little to get a little?" Many of my clients say: "Spend a little, get a lot!" I use e-mail in a targeted way – permission based e-mails. I make sure to ask customers to list my business e-mail address as "allowed". That could be part of your "collection" process – a reminder to "add us to your 'allowed' list to avoid missing our special offers!"

I said there are three steps to growing a business:

1. Bring in new customers

2. Get existing customers to come back more often

3. Get customers to spend more in each transaction

Building your House List is the key for the second component to work.

Unlike those who are blindly advertising for new customers via the older, more traditional media, you can use your House List to generate business. You can also discover who your best customers are. You can see who hasn't been in for some time, and either contact them with a special promotion, or add them into the mailings you are doing in a new customer acquisition strategy.

The House List is an incredibly useful source of information. You can see why I call it your most valuable asset.

CHAPTER 17

The Bounce Back Strategy

Many of the strategies I use to get customers to come back and spend more all piggy back on The Birthday Strategy. I call this one **The Bounce Back Strategy**. When people come in for the birthday promotion (or any promotion for that matter) and they turn in their certificate, you know they've come in and you add them to the House List. What you do next, however, is really unusual and will set your business apart.

I suggest you thank people for coming in and celebrating their birthday with you. Have you ever in your life been thanked by a business just for coming in and getting something for free? You may be thinking: "Of course we thank people for coming in!" but just saying thank you at the till isn't enough. You must mail this thank you to them.

People will think, "Wow! You're thanking me for coming in after getting something for free?"

This doesn't happen in the real world very much so this is why the strategy works so well -- nobody does this. Nobody thanks you in writing, and especially not for taking advantage of a freebie. On top of that provide them *another offer*. Yes, we want them to come back in and by now you understand that to get someone to take an action it takes an offer. In this case it's a lesser offer. Don't give them free service but do provide them more enticement to come in. Since this is something entirely unexpected, it will draw people in. One client of mine recently tried this over a three month period and he got redemptions of over 58%! 58% of the people who came in for their birthday promotion came in a second time within weeks. Amazing!

People enjoy getting something fun in the mail. A thank you is a really pleasant and fun surprise. If you get something in the mail from a company that you've done business with, and you'd be interested in doing business with again, this will elicit a quick response. It's a great strategy to get people back in your door.

There is probably not one in five hundred businesses that would think to do this type of thing.

The power of this strategy is the customers understand you have put some effort and thought into this. Not only did you give them a birthday meal, now you have thanked them for coming in for that birthday meal. Then you gave them something extra: an offer to come back in and see you again. You are touching their heartstrings. Emotions are what "sell" people. It's how they feel about the whole experience concerning your business that determines whether they want to keep doing business with you over and over again.

The thank you is possible because of the printed, personalized certificates that you can easily track. You've got the original list of people to whom you mailed these certificates. You know who came in and redeemed their certificate so now you can execute The Bounce Back Strategy. It works well when done shortly after the original promotion, but you can wait a few weeks. With the tracking system in place you are in control.

There is a good chance that if you can get them in multiple times a high percentage of those people become repeat customers, patrons who continue to return without much further effort on your part. After reading this book though, you won't take these people for granted and not stay in touch with them. You will keep reminding them that you are there on a regular basis, telling them that you appreciate their business and you like seeing them.

Let me share a note with you that I received from Matt, a business owner from Redwood Falls:

"I just wanted to let you know my thoughts on the 2nd step Birthday Follow-up Postcards and I can sum it up in one word "FANTASTIC". It has been a great program with my redemption results approaching 60%. That is an unbelievable number. As you know I have been doing the Birthday Program with you for over 2 years and I have been consistently getting between 38% - 52% redemption every month with that program. Redemption rates like that I had never seen before. Then you came up with the idea to send a Follow-up Thank You Postcard to everyone who redeemed the Birthday Certificate and the redemption rates got even better. The customers love it because they have never been sent a "Thank You" for coming in and getting a FREE Meal on their Birthday before. They feel special because they know that we know they came in. Plus we give them another discount offer to come in again. It builds customer loyalty and repeat business. Of course I love the repeat business."

"The program has been very easy to do as well. You just send me an alphabetical list of clients we send birthday letters to each month in an Excel spreadsheet and I mark a "1" in a column next the name of everyone who redeems the certificate. Just after the end of the month when I have all certificates redeemed I send the list back to you and you sort the names then print and send out the Birthday Follow-Up Postcards from that list. Easy."

"I just want to say thank you for your marketing programs and I would highly recommend them to any business owner."

I never get tired of reading notes like this. I can't wait to read a note hearing how well your promotion goes!

CHAPTER 18

The Half-Birthday Strategy

Have you ever gotten a half-birthday card from anybody? Likely, neither have your customers.

If you understand The Birthday Strategy, you already understand **The Half-Birthday Strategy**. All you have to do is send a mailer out to people six months after they came in for their birthday. Because you track who redeems their certificates you already know who to send these promotions to.

Make this mailer fun! For their half-birthday, send them half a letter in a halved envelope. Yes, you can do this! Check out the example of this at **www.TheCustomerStream.com**. All the same characteristics of the birthday mailer apply -- the handwritten font, live stamp, blind address, etc. -- but when they see an envelope that's been cut in half in their mailbox, they're going to want to open it to see what this crazy person sent to them!

Inside, they will see a letter (you can have fun with its shape too) and they'll recognize it came from your business – the same one they were in six months ago to celebrate their birthday. Hopefully they've come in multiple times since then (and you have tracked that), but whether they visited again or not you have a great chance of getting them to respond to this mailing. This is fun and unique -- nobody sends out half-birthday cards – you will stand out for sure.

This is strictly a "get them in the door again" strategy. You are pulling these names from your House List, specifically from the list of birthday certificates you've collected. This means your costs are minimal and you don't have to make an extremely bold offer like the first time. You often can make a very simple offer with less cost to you and they will still come in. The uniqueness of this approach is an enticement all in itself.

CHAPTER 19

The Thanksgiving Greeting Card Strategy

After Thanksgiving and for the rest of the year people are getting dozens of holiday and Christmas cards. Many businesses will also send out cards in December, which is a nice touch, but with the business of the season and the large volume of mail received these often get lost in the shuffle.

Have you ever considered sending out Thanksgiving greeting cards? **The Thanksgiving Greeting Card Strategy** works well because very few people have ever sent one or received one. Since it's the time of giving thanks, it's a natural reason to mail your House List and thank them and at the same time remind them of your business. No need to worry about standing out from the crowd – because there isn't one. You will once again surprise and entice your customers to come back.

This also works with other lesser known holidays, even those that are made up or extremely obscure. Most people don't know this but in every month of the year there are days that are designated to celebrate or recognize something. Why not have your business "celebrate" these lesser known and obscure holidays?

You could send a card or tie in an offer for things from Library Week (April), to Something-on-a-Stick Day (March 28)! October 5 is National Teacher's Day. There are all sorts of zany ideas you could get from things like Opposite Day or Backward Day (both in late January) – or Lumpy Rug Day in May. (Maybe a "Come in and guess what's under the rug" contest?) You'll find a mind-boggling list at www.holidayinsights.com.

This is all about being creative. Find unique reasons to contact your customers. Obscure holidays are fun and I guarantee that there's not a single business your customers will come across that ever go to these lengths to communicate, appreciate and entertain their customers (unless, of course, they are reading this book too).

CHAPTER 20

The Wow! Experience Strategy

Most of the mailings I have detailed in this book propose a **Wow! Experience** to the customer. This is effective in getting the recipient's attention and response. The mail piece is only part of the Wow! Experience that turns prospects into customers and customers into regular patrons. The service or product you provide, plus your place of business round out The Wow! Experience Strategy and it's critical for getting repeat business.

What makes for a Wow! Experience? For starters, try innovation and exceeding a customer's expectations.

I consult with a lot with restaurants and if you ask any restaurant owner out there they will say they have good food and good service. Honestly, is it really all that much better than the restaurant down the street? Any serious restaurant owner is going to do their best to provide good food and good service. The choice between stopping at one restaurant or another can come down to what side of the street they are on or available parking. There is often nothing that really stands out in most people's minds from one restaurant to another or one business to the next.

You need to be thinking about giving consumers a real reason to come back to **you**, whether you're a restaurateur or chiropractor or dry cleaner or any type of retail or service provider.

What makes **you** stand out from the guy down the street? Are people getting something special or having more fun at your establishment than any other place? What makes you different? Are you paying more attention to them? Do you call your client's by name or even know them? Remembering a person's name is powerful. It makes them feel special to have a business know their name. They will refer to your business as "my place." Seriously.

Are you giving customers something extra? For example, in a restaurant do you give people tiny samples right before they were ready to order dessert? Now they have the taste in their mouth to help them decide. That is something that stands out because it doesn't happen at very many places. What if a dentist calls you after you have had work done to check on how you are feeling? That is something that very few dentists do. It would be the same with a chiropractor if he or his staff followed up with you. The fact that these businesses are going above and beyond what a normal person expects is what makes them memorable. That and excellent service are what give customers or clients the Wow! Experience they are looking for.

Think of what constitutes real value for the customer. Are all your employees trained to the idea of giving more to the customer rather than just up-selling? Are there ways to show you care about your customers?

> *"We see our customers as invited guests to a party, and we are the hosts. It's our job every day to make every important aspect of the customer experience a little bit better."* -- Jeff Bezos, Amazon.com

Atmosphere and background are important. Customers respond to a friendly atmosphere. Your employees' interaction with patrons contributes mightily to this. If you have any business that involves the whole family you should be making sure the kids have a good experience and they will convince their parents to go back there again. That is not to say you shouldn't be giving the parents a good experience too, but kids can have a lot of influence over which businesses the family frequents.

Focus on the little things that make you stand out from everybody else, from innovative marketing to their experience in your place of business. All this contributes to how the customer feels valued.

It pays to think about your clientele and their likely needs and preferences. This can involve or influence the layout or décor of your office. Do you have piped-in music? Is it appropriate for the demographic? Is there something to keep them occupied while they are waiting? This could be a good opportunity for a continuous loop video presentation about your services. Would cookies be appropriate while waiting?

From music to magazines, you need to think long and hard about who comes into your place and whom you want to come into your place. What are their expectations? What are yours? How can you play to your strengths? You want to find ways to target that population with a Wow! Experience that makes them feel comfortable and special.

There is truth to the old saying, "Birds of a feather flock together." Satisfied customers will refer others to.

In today's challenging economy retaining your customer base is critical to your success. It makes sense to go above and beyond to try to keep those existing customers coming back as they are a reliable source of regular and renewable revenue.

Keep in mind the adage: out of sight, out of mind. People get busy. In today's society if you are not reminding people you are there and available and looking to provide for them they will forget about you. You need to exert effort to remind them that you exist and give them reasons to use your services.

If You Don't Give Your

Customers A Wow! Experience,

Your Competitors Will!

CHAPTER 21

The Reward Program and Loyalty Strategy

Successful business owners know it is worth spending some money to get someone as a repeat customer. Besides giving patrons a Wow! Experience, how else can you reward them for their business? Try The Reward Program and Loyalty Strategy.

Signing up customers to a **Rewards Program** is a win-win-win strategy. Many grocery stores have rewards cards. When a patron uses their card they get special prices or incentives on certain items. Some stores have VIP or membership programs that restrict who can shop there. Other rewards programs offer to accumulate points or dollars in an account that the customer can redeem for gifts, free merchandise or free service.

I've noticed many businesses using this strategy quite well. In fact, I would say that customers may be wondering where your Reward Program is if you don't have one. Checking my wallet, I've got cards for two grocery chains, a punch card for the ice cream shop, a wine club card, a coffee card, a hardware store card, a pizza place punch card, a discount card for a local oil change place, a pharmacy card and a membership card for a big-box retailer. Where is yours?

There is a reason that these businesses are using The Reward Program and Loyalty Strategy. How powerful is it that I carry these cards in my wallet? I might carry more if my wallet could hold them! My wife has several more cards in her purse that I don't have room to carry. If you have special privileges or prices at various busi-nesses why in the world would you shop any-where else?

Of course, you must use software to keep track of who is using the program and you should issue cards to your customers that stay in their wallet and remind them to come in and spend. Many of these programs allow you to track when they come in and detail exactly what they spent money on.

Knowing the habits of your customers leads to all kinds of ways to personally cater to them. If you know your customer comes in every two weeks to get ten shirts cleaned why not offer him a special on sport coats or something for his spouse? What about a customer that always stops in and buys sinus medication? You might determine they have an allergy and have all kinds of other products that will help them feel better? What about a customer who comes in every three months for an oil change on their Chevrolet? Sending them a card two weeks before they should come in with a personal greeting and a reminder will insure they remember: "Doug, our records indicate you are due for an oil change on your Chevrolet. Come in by September 30 and get 11% off your service, plus a free top-off on your washer, brake, and transmission fluid." Do you think I would go anywhere else to get my oil changed?

These strategies are designed to encourage customer loyalty and there is no doubt that they work. But as people sign up at each competitor "loyalty" can become relative to the discounts offered. Make sure your offers are strong and personalized and that you actually use the Rewards Program to generate repeat business. If the customers don't receive good value they probably won't return. For instance, I have a VIP card for a large office supply store chain. The only thing they ever send me is an offer to get 25% off my order if I spend over $100. For a big business this might be attractive, but not for my size of business. I rarely use this store or my card. Be careful to not require too much effort or spending to trigger a reward. Asking someone to come in and buy 19 subs to get the 20th free is asking a lot of the customer. Make your rewards and offers easy to obtain. This trains your customers to spend, get a reward and then spend some more.

The Rewards Program Strategy is the ultimate House List. It is not only a list of your customers; it is a list of your *best* customers.

CHAPTER 22

Conclusion

When I discovered Direct Response Marketing (DRM) it transformed my business. Direct Response Marketing not only gives you ways to generate new customers, it gives you the opportunity to generate revenue. The unique and innovative strategies I described in this book will stimulate a stream of customers and will stamp your business's name into a prospect's memory. It takes effort, but keep in mind what that customer can be worth to you in profits over time.

By now, I hope you have visited **www.TheCustomerStream.com** and gone through all the resources I've provided. These strategies are not difficult to implement and the reward is well worth the investment and effort. I trust you have learned from this book how innovation and direct personal contact can result in increased business for you. I hope you see that I didn't hold back on anything here. I've laid out the strategies that have made my clients a lot of money over the years. You just need to follow the processes I laid out.

Perhaps you lack the creativity, time, or organizational skills to get these strategies in place. In that case, find someone who can. Perhaps it's a family member, an employee or marketing professional, but you must find someone to get these in place. These strategies are not worth a dime if they just stay here in this book.

If you want a fast-path to success outsourcing this to someone is the best way. I want you to know that I'm available to work with you on these strategies. Please give me a call at **1-855-693-0699** or e-mail me at **doug@thecustomerstream.com**. I will be more than happy to jumpstart your creativity or develop a campaign with you. I really enjoy brainstorming with clients and coming up with ways to implement these strategies. It feels good to think I have been able to help business owners gain some clarity about how to break out of whatever kind of funk they're in and get some attention through their marketing. I'd love to spend a few minutes with you over the phone discussing these strategies and how I can help you grow your business.

As you have seen, I have a lot of ideas that get your customers to respond. If I can help to get you on the fast-path to success it will be worth your investment. Don't worry. I'm not a high-priced consultant. I know many of you are on a budget, and the economy is tough. I'd like to help you start well and earn some revenue to prove to yourself these strategies work.

I hope to hear from you about your successes and welcome any recommendations or suggestions you may have.

FREE CONSULT!

To speak with Doug Anderson about filling your local business with new customers, getting them to come back, and getting them to spend more money each visit:

Please Call **1-855-693-0699** or Visit **www.TheCustomerStream.com**